Sunshine and Rainbows

By Vaishali Andraskar

Sunshine and Rainbows (Poetry Book)
Copyright © March 2022 Vaishali Andraskar
All rights reserved.

Distributed by: Notion Press, Amazon, Flipkart

ASIN: B09VTJXL78 (Kindle)
ISBN: 9798434649773 (Amazon.com)
ISBN: 9798886298499 (Notion Press)

This is a work of fiction. The characters and events portrayed in this book are fictitious. Any similarity to real persons, living or dead, is coincidental and not intended by the author.

No part of this book may be reproduced, or stored in a retrieval system, or transmitted in any form or by any means, electronic, mechanical, photocopying, recording, or otherwise, without written permission of the author.

Dedicated to my wonderful readers.

Acknowledgments

First and foremost, I would like to thank the Almighty as the lord is the reason we are here today.

I'm eternally grateful to all my mentors without whose inspiring words and guidance this book would not have been possible.

To my family for always being there: Thank you for your support in this first milestone, and many more to come.

About the Author

The author is an award-winning educator working at a reputed school in Pune, India.

She has published two picture books, and her books are available on Amazon and Flipkart. Her poems have been published in various anthologies, and she has received certificates of appreciation for her poetry. She has also participated in open mic sessions, where she has recited her poetry in the presence of seasoned poets and writers.

This book is a collection of her poems with a message of strength and positivity. She hopes that this bouquet of uplifting and thought-provoking poems will entertain you, inspire you, and brighten your day.

Author's note

Poetry is about feelings, emotions, language, measurement, and rhythm. Poetry can be thought-provoking and moving. It can also be inspiring and motivating.

To me, poetry is an art form; it's the freedom to write and paint with words. A poem is mostly like a mirror. You can't see through a mirror; its purpose is to evoke reflection.

This book is a collection of twenty-seven creations, some of which have been previously published in various anthologies. The poems have a short prelude about the topic to help you warm up to the poem. These poems give the message of hope and inspire us to look at the good side of life.

Happy Reading!

CONTENTS

Poems	Page
1. Small things	9
2. The brighter side	12
3. The child in me	16
4. Her wonderful world	19
5. Glory	22
6. Keep going	25
7. Rational or Irrational	28
8. Beyond compare	31
9. Nature – our abode!	34
10. The little paradise	37
11. Wanderlust	40
12. Anticipation	43
13. You make my heart smile	46
14. Power of words	49
15. Unfolding thoughts	52
16. The urban life	55
17. The inner Cinderella	57
18. Simple woman	61
19. Butterflies	65
20. Sometimes	67
21. The skies in the morning	69

22. Pure treasure..72
23. Feelings..75
24. Riverside..76
25. In my dream..79
26. She..83
27. Friend...87

1 Small Things

Small things are actually not so small.

They make up a large part of our lives and matter a lot. They bring joy and their own lessons with them.

And yes, they also help us to form bigger things...

Small things

The mesmerizing dance of the lilies
with the gentle whoosh of wind,
the accentuated colors on Earth
with the light drizzling.

The gleeful rustling of plant leaves
as the sky turned grey,
the pitter-patter sound of raindrops
on the sand and clay.

The soft lightning and light thunder
created music upbeat,
and the earthy scent spread in the air,
appended the treat.

As I witnessed the drama from the window,
immense joy filled my heart.
That instant, I realized how blinded I'd been
to overlook nature's performing art.

Later in the day as I sat in the balcony
with family, sipping coffee,
their wonder-filled eyes watching the sunset
made me smile with glee.

I took a deep breath and appreciated
the moment's pristine beauty.
And reiterated in my mind,
yes, these little things are important to me.

■ First published in 'Elixir of Words Volume III'
May 2021 Edition by 'The Write Order'.

☐☐☐

2 *The brighter side*

Life is not always perfect. Looking at the brighter side of life can help us to be cheerful and optimistic. This constructive energy can help us overcome challenges and difficulties we encounter along the way.

It is also said that a positive outlook has been proven to help heal the body and the mind. Let's give it a try...

The brighter Side

Blank eyes,
bland expressions,
say it all.
The sheer indifference
that people garner
close to heart.

One can feel,
one can see,
the piercing apathy.
The difference
in words and action
that exists in ubiquity.

Integrity and justice,
all seem to be
mere fairy tales.
Discrimination and prejudice
are the ones
which generally prevails.

But remember
humans are mix
of colors and hues
If there are dark ones
that disturb,
you'll find bright ones too.

Just carry on
along the path of truth,
completely focused.
Uplift others
who feel undervalued
and do not let them get deterred.

Look at the
brighter side and have
faith in the power of the divine.
With your sincerity
and determination,
You shall rise and shine!

■ Previously published in the Anthology 'Moonlight'
October 2021 Edition by 'The Write Order'.

□□□

3 The child in me

Children are innately innocent. They have the instinct to love, play, smile, and laugh, inspiring us to follow the same.

And yes, there is a child in every one of us who needs to be revived occasionally.

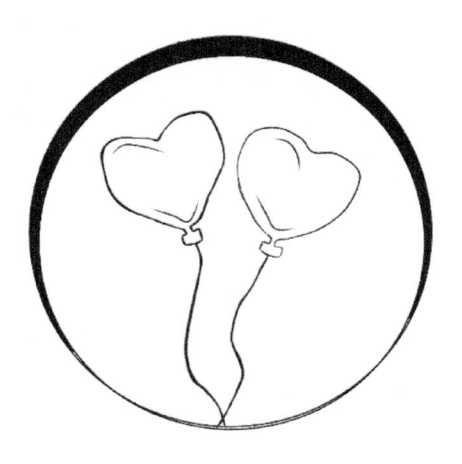

The child in me

The little baby in my hands
stared at me
and smiled intermittently
as I made faces and smiled.
The sweetness of the moment
transpired incomparable
joy in me,
and I felt as happy as a child.

There was just a sweet innocence
I could see;
devoid of any meanness,
selfishness, anger, and hatred.
Only love and trust around,
as the baby fell asleep in my hands,
honoring me in that moment,
which was sacred.

Tears of happiness
welled in my eyes,
filling my heart with tranquility
that we all strive.
I just sat there feeling blessed
and asking myself,
how could I protect
this innocence and joy in life.

I realized over the years,
in the race of adulthood,
I had forgotten the pure,
child-like feelings of love and glee.
I looked at the sleeping baby
and thought,
probably it was now time to
revisit the child in me.

■ Previously published on 'The Passion of Poetry' page and awarded 'Silver Award' in 'Saturday Pix Prompt' dated 13th March 2022, by POP Admin Team.

☐☐☐

4 *Her wonderful world*

In our own little world, we can have everything and feel pure inner joy. It's being with ourselves, without taking much notice of what is going on around us.

We all require our me time. Isn't it?

Her wonderful world

Random thoughts
about the world around her,
flapping like a butterfly,
vivid and soundless.

Casual thoughts
about the world at large,
flying like dry clouds,
pearly and waterless.

Her thoughts and she,
they make an amazing pair.
Her thoughts are not visible,
but they are there.

Venting out her ideas
on lines between the pages,
She feels liberated as she builds,
a unique world of her own.

The wonderful world she creates
on those fluttering pages,
will anyone care about,
she couldn't tell.

But the rhythm created,
the flow of twirling words,
the solace of the moment;
They will all help her celebrate her true
self!

☐☐☐

5 Glory

At times, certain things catch our unsought attention. One of these things may become desirable and the focus of our attention.

But do we need to get and possess everything that we find beautiful and vulnerable?

Glory

In the light breeze at dawn,
swayed the flower of gentle beauty.

It was so charismatic and velvety,
that I wanted to touch it
and feel its smooth pane.

It was so precious and delicate
that I didn't want to touch it,
lest its petals may wane.

But I couldn't ignore it.
It was just so bright and lively.

Wanting to show it to the world,
with my phone, I tried
to click its picture.

But whichever angle I tried,
it was difficult for me
to take a perfect capture.

I realized that a mere picture
couldn't arrest its true beauty.

The fragrant blossom
firmly crowned its prickly stems,
evading the predators.

It was a wonder
to those who could see its charm
and not its creed and color.

The joy was in just letting it be;
Not plucking it, not clicking it.
Just letting it bask in its elegance and glory.

◻◻◻

6 *Keep going*

There are many things that keep us going.

People who are near and dear to us inspire us. Figuring out our goals and remembering them every day, motivates us. Our interests, passion for art and music, as well as our hopes and surprises, encourage us to keep at it.

And if we persevere, we can achieve our goals.

Let's take pleasure in the journey...

Keep going

Believe in yourself and go on.

Just keep trying, and go on.

So much to realize, so much to attain.

So much to try, so much to gain.

If you fall, gather yourself.

If you fail, motivate yourself.

Do not get deterred, just go on.

Do not be disheartened, just go on.

Open your wings, take high strides.

Just be resilient and surf against the tides.

See opportunities in each little thing.

Be grateful for every little blessing.

Be good, be kind and go on.

Live your dreams and go on.

■ Previously published in the Anthology 'Open your wings' December 2021 Edition by Sarvad Publication.

□□□

7   *Rational or Irrational*

Sometimes, it happens that a statement from someone makes you think, and, uh, it's not easy to reason out.

It happened to me too...

Rational or irrational

A student said to me
after my math class.
"Pi is irrational.
Pi is important.
Maybe
being irrational
is not that bad after all."

I just smiled but was surprised
by the statement.
And the way this concept applies
to our real world,
where we encounter irrationality,
though the percentage is small.

Most of the time,
we humans are rational,
with the ability to think, act and adapt
to our surroundings.
But, as you would agree,
Irrationality
does exist.

Though there is no
clear demarcation as such.
With our obsessions, phobias,
and prejudices,
at times,
we all have irrational thoughts
and conflicts.

Nevertheless,
we need a balance of both.
And that's what
makes us human, probably.

Maybe
being irrational
is not that bad after all…

Could be.

□□□

8 *Beyond compare*

All of us have experienced unexpected connections with someone we just met, at some point in life.

Though difficult to explain, these connections can turn into deeper bonds, creating special and delightful moments.

Beyond Compare

Some people seek
rhyme and reason,
some others are skeptical
and they question.

>Prying eyes, frown,
>when we have fun like crazy.
>Maybe they wonder about
>our casual connection.

>No, they're not wrong
>in looking for some rationale
>and a common ground for
>our bonding and equation.

But I'm happy that some
friendships are pure and honest,
and not based merely on
return and expectation.

> It's not for how long
> we've known each other.
> But sometimes the immediate
> connection happens, though rare.

> > I cherish such associations
> > and feel they're destined.
> > For me, unexpected bonds are
> > the best and beyond compare!

■ Previously published in 'Unexpected Bonds' Anthology by Sarvad Publication.

☐☐☐

9 Nature – our abode

The word 'nature' brings up so many thoughts, feelings, and emotions in us. There are many lessons too, which we can learn from nature.

Here's a slightly different poem on nature - a concrete poem...

Nature – our abode!

Note: The concrete poem is on the next page (page no. 33). It is not just a poem, but it surely is a poem.

Concrete poetry (also known as shape poetry) is formed by patterns of words, letters, or symbols rather than the usual arrangement of words.

You may start reading from the first word 'be' and read linearly (line wise), just as you would read a traditional poem.

Be
one
with
nature   as
it's   pristine   and
truly   relaxing   always.
Nature is part of us and we are
part of it, nature is healing and
kindly giving all the days.
Feel the fresh breeze,
listen to the rustling of leaves, chirping
of birds, just revel in the warmth
of tender, soothing sun rays.

Nature	!	our world;
it's	!	our
abo-	!	-de!

☐☐☐

10 *The little paradise*

Paradise is a very beautiful, gratifying, and harmonious place that seems perfect.

For some, paradise on earth might be where they have peace of mind. For others, it might be a place where all live in harmony. For some others, it might be watching the sunset, or a rainbow, or just being one with nature.

What is your concept of paradise on earth?

The little paradise

The gusty winds and frenzied drops
plummeted on the roof with force.
The graying skies and gloomy weather
pestered me to stay indoors.

As the rain pounded relentlessly,
I pulled in the curtains and had a cozy tea.
Then watched the news for some time
and painted on canvas, getting artsy.

As the thunderclaps mellowed
and shifted to a serene drizzle,
I slowly pulled the curtains aside,
only to reveal, a breath-taking marvel.

On the giant luminescent canvas
of the seamless blue sky,
a miraculously iridescent rainbow
arched clear and high.

From my apartment window, I could see,
wet roads and trees with reddish blossom.
A cityscape, creating an art display,
complementing the spectrum.

I stared awestruck at the beauty,
my eyes twinkling with childlike mirth.
Not that I hadn't seen it all before,
but felt, I witnessed little paradise on Earth.

Though it was fleeting and ephemeral,
The rainbow touched the core.
And who'll not be happy with the vibrant crescent,
which brings cheer after a dreary downpour.

■ Previously published in the Anthology 'Paradise' October 2021 Edition, by 'The Write Order'.

☐☐☐

11 *Wanderlust*

At times, we wish to travel to a faraway place, and it may not be possible at that time due to restrictions (as during lockdown) or other conditions.

So, we just visualize the place, discuss it with others, read about it, or opt for a virtual tour, and embark on our journey...

Wanderlust

The moon wanders
day and night.
Merrily spinning around
the wandering earth,
spreading its divine light.

Commoners are wanderers too,
with wandering eyes.
Cotton masks in place,
a sanitizer in the bag,
and a travel book besides.

Merrily they move around
with wandering feet.
From home to workplace
and back,
to make both ends meet.

Back at home,

after the chores,

the television takes

wandering minds

to unseen lush outdoors.

When commoners long,

but can't adjust.

Their daily commute

and the virtual trips,

helps gratify their wanderlust.

■ Previously published in the Anthology Wanderlust' in November 2021 Edition by 'The Write Order'.

☐☐☐

12 *Anticipation*

Anticipation is an action of expecting what might be. It is to foresee and expect an event that is most likely to happen.

We can anticipate promotion in our jobs, a movie to be good enough or a justifiable holiday after a hectic work schedule.

It is best to open our minds to possibilities and do our best for the best possible outcomes.

Anticipation

The river meanders
gracefully, but restlessly,
envisioning its dramatic
meeting with the ocean.

The moon grows
sliver to half, half to full,
longing to see the zealous tides
who reciprocate the emotion.

Day anticipates night
and night anticipates the day,
and every moment waits for
the next moment in eager expectation.

Things keep happening

maybe or not as per the assumption.

Yet the present anticipates the future

and the world keeps going in anticipation.

■ Previously published on 'The Passion of Poetry' page and awarded 'Certificate of Excellence in 'Member's Choice Mondays' dated 28th January 2022, by POP Admin Team.

☐ ☐ ☐

13 *You make my heart smile*

In our lives, we have certain people with whom we like to spend our time. Time flies when we are in this good company, as they make us happy and ignite our inner joy.

Think of the person who creates such emotion in you, as you warm up to this Acrostic poem…

You make my heart smile

Years passed by, my friend, and how I wonder;
our friendship managed to remain
untouched and pure.

Many so-called friendships lie bare now,
alone true friendship, as ours lasts.
Keeping magical moments,
etched and treasured in our hearts.

My friend, such a beauty
you have been.
Honest eyes,
Ever understanding smile,
And the warmth of your presence
Reassuring me about your affection;
Trusting me with all these therein.

Sometimes I feel, friendship is like a poem,
made for those who see its beauty and go the extra mile;
It dwells in the heart and has its rhythm,
liberating in the true sense, with no ifs and buts,
everlasting and making our hearts smile.

☐☐☐

14 *Power of words*

Words are powerful. Writing or expressing thoughts with the right words has the power to influence people, even far and wide.

Power of words

Sometimes, words are like pearls.

They string up to show love and care.

Sometimes, words are like winter.

They leave you cold and bare.

Sometimes, words are like a rainbow

They simply brighten up your day.

Sometimes words are like an arrow

they cause quiet hurt and ache.

Words do make a difference,

As they provide our emotions an outlet.

Words have the power to influence

even the people we never met.

Words should be used carefully

to harness the good around us

Words make an impact forever

Boundless is the power of words.

■ Previously published on 'The Passion of Poetry' page and awarded 'Honorable mention' in 'Member's Choice Mondays' dated 19th February 2022, by POP Admin Team.

□□□

15 *Unfolding thoughts*

Every so often, most of us just relax with a cup of tea/coffee in hand, thinking about life and reflecting on certain things.

Who knows, these thoughts might just unfold some of the minutiae which we might have not realized earlier…

Unfolding thoughts

Note: The concrete poem is on the next page (page no. 51). It is not just a poem, but it surely is a poem.

Concrete poetry is formed by patterns of words, letters, or symbols rather than the usual arrangement of words.

You may start reading linearly (line-wise), just as you would read a traditional poem.

She smiled amazed
at how their bonding had
strengthened and improved,
with passing time and over the years.
Whilst just at the start of their journey
she was coolly told by her so-called friends
that after the marriage usually, out of the window,
all love, trust and care simply disappears.
She felt It might differ person to person;
the key was to hold on to make it work,
to be there for each other everytime,
and to show that each one cares.
As she thought of the times when,
he took efforts to see her happy,
times when she stood by him,
times when he first said sorry
after a tiff and also times
she spoke nothing,
but he was all ears.
She wondered how they
were never vocal about their love,
But their affectionate eyes gave it out,
And to her this magic of love is that endears.

◻◻◻

16 *The urban life*

Life in a metropolitan city is a flurry of activities. This comes with its own set of benefits and challenges.

Here's a haiku chain on city life.

A haiku is traditionally a Japanese poem consisting of three short lines that do not rhyme. A haiku chain is a series of linked poems.

the urban life

with high-rise buildings,
and the shanties side-by-side,
urban jungle thrives.

workday rush at dawn
back home amid city lights
impassive urban lives

active virtual life
a loud say on all issues
whether truth or lies

to tackle the challenge
of social welfare and growth,
the urban life strives

four trees, forty vehicles
causing air pollution woes
yet city survives

□□□

17 The inner Cinderella

We have been raised to act composed and presentable, with our guard intact as expected by society. We match our inner self with these expectations and so people rarely notice our true inner self.

But is it necessary to always conform to the norms of the community? Or can we set ourselves loose at times, living our true selves, channelling the inner Cinderella, or the Prince?

The inner Cinderella

She was not her,
in the moment;
without any inhibition
she danced to the rhythm.
The pair of eyes
that moved along her
did not matter to her.

She was not her,
in that moment;
her moves glistened like water,
her curves highlighted like waves,
the fluid motion at the blink of an eye,
the ruffle of rebellious folds of her attire
did not seem to deter her.

She was not her
some eyes widened,
some eyes narrowed,
what happened to her
some faces frowned.
But she felt free
as she hadn't felt ever before.

She was not her
the pearl had come
out of its shell
her aura shone
like a stunning crystal
she was unbelievable
and not any of her.

There wasn't any fairy Godmother
to help her get to the party,
to get her the Prince
whom she wanted to please.
So she set herself loose
owning every moment
and living her fairy tale dreams.

Just then the music stopped
totally stunning her
making her aware.
She moved aside and walked out
wrapped in her familiar blanket
of shyness and uneasiness;
a small smile on her face.

□□□

18 Simple woman

A simple woman is not superficial, not complicated. She values relations and has simple personality traits.

Do you have such a woman in your life?

Simple Woman

Behind the façade,
behind the commotion,
you can find me.
I am a simple woman.

From my birth to puberty,
and giving birth to my old age;
I try to be flawless
in all that I attempt to be.
I fail, at times
but still, I strive to be perfect,
trying to avoid exploitation,
trying to please everybody.

Behind the façade,
behind the commotion,
you can find me.
I am a simple woman.

The hype is about the movement,
looking at women as independent
and strong career persons,
who hog the limelight to a great degree.
And here I am, sometimes unable to decide
if I am a working woman or a housewife,
frayed between taking care of kids
and going to work daily.

Behind the façade,
behind the commotion,
you can find me.
I am a simple woman.

I wish good for my people.
And I cook, clean, and mop the floor.
I also try to be presentable,
and try to conform to society.
I try to be a good homemaker,
while doing something for my own self,
sometimes out of passion,
sometimes to aid home with extra money.

Behind the façade,
behind the commotion,
you can find me.
I am a simple woman.

I may have my vulnerabilities.
I may have my insecurities.
And I may be not-so-good;
For I may judge other women blatantly.
And I may be mean to other women too.
Yet I have friends and we enjoy together.
I travel and do things I love,
And that makes me ME.

Behind the façade,
behind the commotion,
you can find me.
I am a simple woman.

□□□

19   *Butterflies*

Butterflies are the plant pollinators and markers of a healthy ecosystem. They are beautiful and special in their own way.

Yet, it is not quite often that we pause and notice the beauty of these tiny little creatures. And if we do, they stir up joy from within.

Here's a haiku (chain) on butterflies…

Butterflies

Pretty butterflies.
Flapping their colorful wings,
hunting the nectar.

Flimsy butterflies.
Yet, they soften even the
hardened up people.

Divine butterflies,
with their striking symmetry
and alluring patterns.

Crucial butterflies.
Yet so simple and humble;
they make us wonder.

Resolute butterflies.
Their wings tell the tale of struggle;
cocoon to adult.

Pretty butterflies.
Flapping their colorful wings,
hunting the nectar.

☐☐☐

20 *Sometimes*

Sometimes we get tired of carrying the baggage of goodness around us.

Though we might feel that being good is the right thing to do.

Still, sometimes it happens so…

Sometimes ...

Sometimes I get exhausted

of this whole goodness pretense.

For, however, I try from my side,

no assurance; I'll get goodness in return.

Sometimes I get weary

of virtues learned as a child.

For, in the real world these virtues,

do exist, but are tricky to find.

Sometimes I just breathe

in my goodness and simplicity.

It's my courage built over the years,

and not my incompetency.

Sometimes I just carry on

pushing off the weariness and grumble.

Trying to rekindle my belief in kindness,

and being good to good people.

☐☐☐

21 *The skies in the morning*

While taking a morning walk in a park, we witness the birdsongs and the fresh air, feeling calm and serene.

The daybreak is energizing, and simply beautiful.

The skies in the morning

The just-rising sun
amidst the silvery clouds,
spreading the pure light
with its golden fingers.
The mix of blues, reds, greys
and pinks cast in the skies,
and the feel of a cool breeze
along with the dawn chorus that lingers.

The early morning skies enchant us
with their unique glow,
their varying patterns,
and the multitude of shades.
But with speeding time,
the sun emerges entirely,
augmenting the blue,
and the other hues fades.

The skies in the morning are
a work of art by the supreme artist.
Overlooked due to morning activities,
but indeed, a great blessing.
They remind us to be grateful
for the new prospects.
And to open new horizons,
while doing our own thing.

Just take time to appreciate
the endless love and connection,
and take pleasure
in nature's humble joys;
To realize that no matter
how different our horizons are,
still, we are connected
and bound by the same skies.

☐☐☐

22 *Pure treasure*

What are the things that we treasure in life?

There are actually so many! All small and big things are a treasure, for which we are grateful.

One such priceless treasure is true friendship. If we are fortunate enough to have true friends, we have a pure treasure that would last for a lifetime…

Pure Treasure

I interact with many,
but share thoughts,
and chatter a lot
with only a few.

I've similarities with many,
but valuing differences,
and enduring concurrences
is important to only a few.

I laugh out with many,
but cracking up at nothing,
and having fun in everything
is possible with only a few.

I know many attractive people,
but people beautiful inside - out
about whom blindly I can vouch
are only a few.

In hours of need and joy
and situations otherwise
the ones who'll be on my side
are only a few.

Besties, comrades, confidant,
well-wisher, pal, or supporter.
Call them by any name,
they are pure treasure.

All these amazing people
are lifeline and a necessity.
I just hope that they resonate
with the same sentiments about me.

■ Previously published in 'The Leverage in words' August 2021 Edition by 'The Write Order'.

☐☐☐

23   Feelings

We, humans, are a product of our emotions and feelings.

But there are times when people try to conceal their feelings.

Do you relate to such situations?

Feelings

ignore me if you will
just pass by if you wish
do not speak if you must

just don't make that mistake.
don't look at me.

for
your eyes
are not trained
to contain
the volume
of your feelings

they give out the days
you looked through me
and also
the nights you spent
thinking of me.

□□□

24   *Riverside*

We feel pleasant around the water bodies and throng the waterfalls, beaches, pools, and lakes.

Rivers also hold our attention and awaken deep emotions in us.

Riverside

it was an evening beside a mountain river.

    the river burbled and roared,
    streaming down the slope,
    speaking to me.

    the greyish-white river curved
    amidst the forested sideways
    and the twittering birds.

    it turned
    and twisted along,
    paving its way.

    up-close
    i could sense
    its whistling in the wind,
    and chuckling
    against the tickling rocks.

the serenity,

the rawness

struck me

at that moment.

i stood awed,

happy that the river was

still untouched.

not asked to mind its trail

not asked to control its hysterics

unrestrained

and

unpolluted.

unlike the others.

☐☐☐

25   *In my dream*

Dreaming about magic may seem illusory to us. But they sometimes reveal our feelings to ourselves.

Have you had such a dream lately?

In my dream

In my dream, I saw a mystical door
surrounded by pearly, shining clouds.
A sweet, soulful musical beat
resonated in the air, somewhere nearabouts.

Amazed by the magical glitter and
the sweet fragrance, I tip-toed to the door.
I slowly peeped in through it,
to the magical world, only to get floored.

There awaited a spectacle,
which made me stumble in delight.
The Moon and the stars danced,
hand in hand, in that magical night.

The deep blanket of black cosmos and the sprinkling of dreamy shiny light through millions of stars.
The diamonds, the magical pixie dust sprinkled around them, kept me in awe.

The Moon swung from star to star, displaying graceful moves.
The stars twirled, swirled, and whirled, with sensuous grooves.

I rubbed my eyes and pinched myself, I knew it was not true.
It was probably that I was tipsy with thoughts of you.

It was only a pleasant dream, which 1 would
like to behold together.
And marvel at the cosmic party along with
you each night, forever.

☐☐☐

26 *She*

Occasionally, having a dialogue with one's internal self is important.

Inspired by the subconscious mind, this discourse may help vent our hidden thoughts, beliefs, and doubts.

She

Gazing in the mirror
wondered she.
Is this just a body
or soulful me?

Her reflection laughed slyly,
taking her by surprise.
'What makes you ponder?'
it asked her, with prying eyes.

Her eyebrows crinkled and she half-smiled,
"My color, looks, size, and waist girth;
Often, the appearance of me
decides my worth!"

The reflection smiled as it said
"What others think, does it really amount?
Isn't it, what you think about yourself,
and, your mind and courage that counts?"

"Yeah, it's kind of true," she exhaled.
"But is it wrong to want to be accepted?
Even if fat, even if skinny, or whatever,
without feeling discriminated."

"Not really; but life is not always
rainbows and sunshine," the reflection said.
"Not everything will go your way,
Let go and keep moving ahead."

Her eyes lit with affirmation,
"Yes, I realize, but still sometimes it hurts.
The so-called standards of disguised lives,
creates feelings of discomfort."

"Avoid trying to please others",
the reflection said in a calm voice.
"You are far more than your body,
claiming what's yours, is your choice."

The reflection concluded fading gradually,
"Just focus on your aspirations.
It's a long way dear,
do not lose heart yet!"

Gazing in the mirror
marveled she.
Is this just a body
and not soulful me?

◻◻◻

27 *Friend*

We have many people around us whom we consider our friends.

Also, it is good to make new friends from time to time.

But it can be challenging to connect with new people and place our trust in them.

Friend

It was just that our eyes met;
as she entered the office room
and stood aside.
From across the room she
kept looking at me
probably trying to gauge my frame of mind.

Things weren't going my way that day
and I was a bit upset, and hurt.
But I wanted to keep it to myself
and never spoke out a word.

Still, she slowly came near me
and stood beside.
"All, okay?", she asked softly
taking me by surprise.

I sulked more, feeling vulnerable,
my eyes looking for an emotional outpour.
She held my hand sensing my feelings,
and waiting for me to get my hold.

She touched my heart as
she cared to stop and comfort,
It took some time, but I opened
my heart to her and felt better.

As I thanked her,
she reminded me of an instance.
When I had comforted
her sometime back.

I couldn't actually remember
of any such event.
But as she said, "See you",
while moving away,
I knew I had a friend.

■ Previously published on 'The Passion of Poetry' page and awarded 'Certificate of Excellence in 'Saturday Pix Prompt' in August 2002, by POP Admin Team.

☐☐☐

Thank you for your support. If you liked the book kindly recommend it to a friend.

You may also leave a review on Amazon/ Flipkart or send your feedback to vaishaliandraskar21@gmail.com.

Printed in Great Britain
by Amazon